For Your Garden

ORNAMENTAL GRASSES

For Your Garden
ORNAMENTAL GRASSES

Text and Principal Photography by
RICK DARKE

BARNES
&NOBLE
BOOKS
NEW YORK

ISBN 0-7607-0503-8

M 10 9 8 7 6 5 4 3 2 1

Editor: Kelly Matthews
Art Directors: Jeff Batzli and Lynne Yeamans
Designer: Stan Stanski
Photography Director: Christopher C. Bain

Color separations by Fine Arts Repro House Co., Ltd.
Printed and bound in China by Leefung-Asco Printers Ltd.

Table of Contents

INTRODUCTION
6

Chapter One
THE UNIQUE BEAUTY OF ORNAMENTAL GRASSES
8

Chapter Two
FORMAL LANDSCAPES
20

Chapter Three
INFORMAL LANDSCAPES
30

Chapter Four
GRASSES IN NATIVE LANDSCAPES
42

Chapter Five
CONTRASTING ELEMENTS
48

INDEX
72

INTRODUCTION

*U*nique among garden plants, ornamental grasses have a special relationship with nature. Whether dancing and glistening in the late afternoon sun, swaying sensuously with the gentlest summer breeze, or melodiously rustling by the edge of a pond, grasses respond with unparalleled intimacy to the subtle changes of the seasons, delightfully intensifying an appreciation of the natural life cycle of the garden.

Offering both beauty and hardiness, today's palette of ornamental grasses includes myriad variations in size, form, texture, and color with grasses available to suit almost any purpose in the garden. Diminutive gems can serve as delicate garden accents, while midsize species can fill niches commonly reserved for specimen shrubs or hedges, and the tallest species, growing as much as fifteen feet (4.5m) in a single season, can have the presence of small trees. Shapes and forms also run the full gamut, with strictly upright grasses perfect for creating dramatic exclamation points, gently arching types useful for connecting adjacent plantings, and low spreaders offering superb ground cover possibilities. In addition, grass textures cover a wide range, from as coarse as corn to as fine as feathers. The spectrum of grass colors is also broad, with snow white, pearlescent pink, and purple-bronze blooms lasting from midsummer through autumn. When sun-dried, the flowers become silvery plumes that frequently remain attractive throughout winter. Foliage colors of countless tones of green, white, yellow, blue, and red make an appearance in summer, followed by an autumn array of golds, burnt-umbers, and burgundies.

Ornamental grasses are among the easiest to grow of all perennial plants. Although the majority prefer sunny sites, they are otherwise adaptable to a wide range of soil, temperature, and moisture conditions and are relatively disease- and pest-free. Their fibrous root systems are very efficient, making most grasses extremely drought tolerant. For the most part, maintenance consists of a once-yearly cutting back, plus occasionally dividing the plants to renew vigor.

Whether your garden is modest or vast, formal or informal, or in a dry or rainy climate, the beauty, diversity, and ease of gardening with ornamental grasses offer splendid opportunities to increase your gardening pleasure.

ABOVE: The silvery plumes of ravenna grass, *Erianthus ravennae*, shoot skyward in mid-autumn, silhouetted by the sun.

OPPOSITE: Stripped of their seeds by winter's end, plumes of *Miscanthus* 'Graziella' are fixed in a gentle wave.

Chapter One

THE UNIQUE BEAUTY OF ORNAMENTAL GRASSES

By gardening with ornamental grasses, a gardener's focus must naturally shift slightly away from color, and emphasis must be placed on such features as translucency, line, form, texture, scale, variegation, and seasonal interest. By developing a sensitivity to the unique attributes of grasses and using their features to their full advantage in the blueprint or planning stages of your garden, you will reap the most rewards when gardening with these unusual plants. As a rule of thumb, grasses are particularly effective when backlit by the sun; their translucent foliage and flowers shimmer and

glow. Although a few grasses are wide-leaved and bold, most have strong-lined, narrow foliage that provides stunning contrast to broad-leaved companion plants. In addition, grasses are at their best when intermingled with other types of perennials and with shrubs and trees. Most remain effective long after the growing season ends; their splendid autumn tones weather gracefully to winter hues of chestnut, fawn, and russet, making them ideal neighbors to brightly berried shrubs and trees with ornamental bark. Allow the grasses to extend your garden's appeal throughout the year.

ABOVE: Side-lit by the autumn sun, the narrow plumes of feather-reed grass, *Calamagrostis* 'Karl Foerster', glow like candles. This grass retains its delicate translucency through winter, when the streaming rays of the sun strike a low angle. Coaxed by the wind, individual plumes move in and out of the sun streams, creating a magical flickering effect.

OPPOSITE: The flowers of mellic grass, *Melica ciliata*, are brilliantly illuminated when backlit by the early summer sun. The shadows behind the plant provide a dark contrast and enhance the radiance of the flowers, adding depth and texture to the scene.

TOP: Strong lines drawn by the foliage of grasses are most effective when contrasted against dark spaces or bold objects. Here, creating a stunningly crosshatched natural window frame, the daggerlike leaves of porcupine grass, *Miscanthus* 'Strictus', reveal just enough of the view beyond to excite the imagination.

ABOVE: The variegated foliage of this *Miscanthus* 'Morning Light' creates a flowing fountainlike effect that epitomizes the graceful beauty of ornamental grasses. The finely linear foliage of the grass is strikingly juxtaposed with its broad-leafed and bold-textured companions.

LEFT: The coarse texture and large scale of giant reed, *Arundo donax*, make this grass an appropriate match for this distinctive English dwelling. The grass boldly competes with the large flowers of the hydrangea, and the plant's upright, vertical growth creates a nice counterpoint to the vine trailing horizontally in the background.

ABOVE: Oblique lighting accentuates the dramatic form of this tall moor grass, *Molinia* 'Karl Foerster'. Dense and irregular in shape, the backdrop of richly textured conifers showcases the ordered filaments of the grass, seemingly holding the grass flowers aloft. Although this arrangement is painted entirely in greens, it has great depth and contrast.

ABOVE: Color can be the most compelling aspect of some grasses. Here, the teal foliage of this fescue, *Festuca* 'Meerblau', combines with the carmine and pink-flowered heathers to create a beautiful palette of ground covers. The tufted mounds of the grass are also complemented by the carefree form of the heather.

LEFT: This ribbon of Japanese bloodgrass, *Imperata* 'Red Baron', mixed with variegated meadow foxtail, *Alopecurus pratensis* 'Variegatus', creates an exuberant, arresting border.

ABOVE: Variegated grasses offer exciting opportunities for brightening secluded, shady corners or providing distinct focal points in garden compositions. Here, the classic symmetry of variegated giant reed, *Arundo donax* 'Variegata', creates a piece of living sculpture.

OPPOSITE: Stirring gently in a summer breeze, dancing before an autumn storm, or flying in a spring gale, grasses mirror nature's moods, bringing a special dynamism to the garden. Here, New Zealand grasses paint a portrait in the wind.

OPPOSITE: The platinum and silver plumes of ornamental grasses make ideal companions for the brilliant autumn foliage of deciduous trees and shrubs. Here, pampas grass, *Cortaderia selloana*, enhances the rich scarlet of a mountain ash.

ABOVE: Many grasses are wondrously colored in autumn. Although green in summer, the leaves of this wild oat, *Chasmanthium latifolium*, become golden licks of flame in autumn, and the intricate detail of the oatlike seed-heads is marvelously revealed by the late-season backlighting.

ABOVE AND RIGHT: Frost follows the graceful lines of these mixed grasses in two views of a steel-gray English morning. Nodding heads of thistles echo the grasses' cascading foliage, and dark tree trunks create an aura of intrigue and mystery. Few garden plants meet the end of the growing season with such serene beauty.

ABOVE: The rigors of winter fail to diminish the magnificence of ornamental grasses. Encrusted with ice in a late-winter storm, this *Miscanthus* drips with jewel-like crystals.

LEFT: This *Miscanthus* seed-head emerged in late summer as a flag of coppery flowers, matured through autumn into a downy plume, and closed winter as this stunning filigree. Although the seed-head is delicate, its life could be further extended if used in an arrangement of dried flowers.

Chapter Two

FORMAL LANDSCAPES

*D*iverse in form and function, ornamental grasses are equally at home in formal and informal garden designs. Although there is no definitive distinction between the two styles, formal landscapes are usually characterized by orderly plantings often built around distinct axes or symmetries. In formal designs, grasses may be used as focal points, as specimens for accent, or in ordered sweeps or patterns.

RIGHT: Grasses are often at their best near water. With its rounded form artfully fitted to the curve of the stone coping, this magnificent specimen of *Miscanthus* 'Morning Light' makes a stunning focal point for a corner of an elegant pool. The finely variegated cascading foliage is subtly mirrored in the still water, surrounded by the billowy reflections of the nearby trees.

OPPOSITE: In this interior courtyard, lush sweeps of *Molinia* and *Sesleria* flow effortlessly behind the curvilinear design of a retaining wall, creating a living sea of green. In the foreground, the tawny heads of *Koeleria* resemble a miniature prairie. Even though the space is modest and the planting is highly ordered, the fine texture and inherent detail of the grasses give the visual impression of a vast landscape with a sense of natural abandon.

ABOVE: The blue-gray foliage of blue oat grass, *Helictotrichon sempervirens*, makes a handsome combination with the low formal hedge of 'Crimson Pygmy' barberry. This duo has great staying power, since both plants retain their foliage color from spring through late autumn. The oat grass will add its delicate flower spikes to the scene in early summer; however, in this mid-spring view, the floral interest is provided by pink-purple tulips interplanted with the grass. Many bulbs, such as crocuses and daffodils, coexist happily with ornamental grasses. After the bulbs flower in the spring, their foliage is neatly masked by the subsequent growth of the grasses.

LEFT: In this art-form California garden, the single fountain grass, *Pennisetum alopecuroides*, serves a sculptural purpose, its rounded form mimicking the bluish yuccas. The sweeps of succulents and sharp turns of the walls and planting beds impart an austere, angular feeling to the design, with the grass adding a welcome softness.

ABOVE: A classic greensward and close-clipped evergreens define these highly formal flower borders, yet the patch of tufted hair grass, *Deschampsia cespitosa*, seems quite appropriate to the design. Airy and cloudlike, the straw-colored flowers of the grass add levity to the ordered landscape and accentuate the sculpted beauty of the evergreens and the antique urn.

LEFT: An intimate path leads to this hidden pool surrounded by Japanese umbrella pines. This secret garden is graced by a river of purple barberry flowing down a slope, leading the eye to focus on a large specimen of fountain grass, *Pennisetum alopecuroides*, nestling against a tall *Iris pseudacorus*. Although neither is in flower, the contrasting forms and textures of these two plants make for a beautifully balanced composition.

OPPOSITE: The tall lines of this variegated giant reed, *Arundo donax* 'Variegata', provide a boldly formal focal point in an otherwise loosely planted courtyard garden.

ABOVE: This exuberant studio garden makes delightful use of annuals, perennials, and tender species to create a richly colored composition. Short and tufted blue fescue, *Festuca ovina* var. *glauca*, and tall and feathery blue oat grass, *Helictotrichon sempervirens*, contribute exquisite steel-blues to the palette.

LEFT: A magnificent specimen of golden variegated pampas grass, *Cortaderia* 'Gold Band', anchors this traditional English-style flower border. The brightly striped foliage of the grass is in perfect harmony with the border's yellow color scheme, and the cascading foliage contrasts effectively with the vertical flower spikes of the silver mulleins.

ABOVE LEFT: The massive trunks of Chilean wine palms contribute to the otherworldly feeling of this Southern California garden. The pervading color scheme is carried successfully from alternating ground cover sweeps of blue senecio and the lower mounds of blue fescue grass, *Festuca ovina* var. *glauca*, to the fan-shaped leaves of blue hesper palms above.

ABOVE RIGHT: This contemporary garden in Japan consists almost entirely of sculpted evergreen trees and shrubs. Although much of the garden is shaded in late afternoon, sunbeams brightly illuminate the copper flowers of a specimen *Miscanthus*, which serves as the central unifying element in the garden's design. Native to Japan, *Miscanthus* is a traditional Japanese emblem of autumn.

OPPOSITE TOP: The bold-textured flowers of purple clematis in this English border are perfect foils for the feathery plumes of *Pennisetum villosum*, the brightest white of all the fountain grasses. The ample width of the stone paving allows the grass to spill voluptuously into the walkway.

OPPOSITE BOTTOM: This sunken garden combines a formally symmetrical paving design with relatively unstructured plantings, evoking the romanticism of a garden ruin. Although there are a number of ornamental grasses in the picture, they are discreetly and effectively incorporated into the composition. Some serve as focal points, others provide fine-textured contrast, and still others are employed solely for the color of their foliage.

Chapter Three

INFORMAL LANDSCAPES

*I*nherently informal, the flowing foliage of ornamental grasses and the carefree abandon of their
flowers often seem ideal choices when the design intent is to
create a casual mood, subtly suggestive of natural,
unstudied landscapes.

RIGHT: On a hazy midsummer's day, this
understated border plays gently with the sun-
light and gracefully meets the pastoral landscape beyond. The bold forms of purple coneflower and globe thistle are distinct against the
soft mass of switch grass, *Panicum virgatum.*
Behind the grass, sedums and the orbicular
foliage of giant coneflower provide additional
textural variety.

OPPOSITE: Grasses and sedges consort in
seemingly random fashion around this small
naturalistic pond. The dark sheet of water balances the airiness of the grasses while the water
lilies contrast with the grass foliage in both
form and texture. The rough-hewn stones edg-
ing the pond contribute to the casual mood,
adding to the illusion that this garden is an
uncontrived part of the native landscape.

ABOVE: This late-autumn glimpse of the border shown on the previous page details its magical transformation into a vibrantly colored tribute to the season. At left, the switch grass, *Panicum virgatum*, has turned golden yellow, as have the leaves of the giant coneflower. *Miscanthus* 'Purpurascens' is now the star of the border, and its dark orange foliage and silvery plumes are stunning in combination with the blackish seed-heads of the coneflower and the rich wine color of the sedum.

RIGHT: Ingeniously placed grasses lend a naturalness and intimacy to this backyard patio that belie the garden's semi-urban location. The fine texture of porcupine grass, *Miscanthus* 'Strictus', is particularly effective in association with the large leaves of the plume poppy and the dark tree trunks.

ABOVE: Ornamental grasses can be employed to create a natural screen, blocking unwanted views or restructuring garden spaces in much the same way a hedge or shrub border might be used. Here, a semi-circular sweep of feather-reed grass, *Calamagrostis* 'Karl Foerster', defines a private space under the spreading branches of a honey locust, providing a delightful spot for outdoor dining.

ABOVE AND RIGHT: Identical views of the same garden taken one month apart dramatically illustrate the alchemy of perennial borders that include a mixture of ornamental grasses. In early summer (*above*), floral fountains of mellic grass, *Melica ciliata*, adorn the rustic stone path while pink roses reach their blooming peak. Later (*right*), the mellic grass assumes a minor role in a tapestry of greens as a river of blue lyme grass, *Elymus arenarius*, rises to become a focal point accompanied by bright yellow daylilies.

ABOVE: The subtle foliage and flower colors of dormant grasses provide a matchless background for displaying the subdued winter hues of companion plants. A tawny background sweep of *Miscanthus* beautifully sets off the striped foliage and intricate seed pods of variegated yuccas.

OPPOSITE: Tucked behind seed-heads of orange coneflower in a tiny urban garden, this feather-reed grass, *Calamagrostis* 'Karl Foerster', is dazzlingly illuminated by just a few sun rays threading through the leaves of a neighboring maple.

ABOVE: As companion flowers ebb and flow, this border is continually brightened by a spreading mass of ribbon grass, *Phalaris arundinacea* 'Picta'.

OPPOSITE: A huge specimen of silver feather grass, *Miscanthus* 'Silberfeder', is magnificently framed by dark green conifers. The cascading form of the grass gives it particular charm.

ABOVE: Pampas grasses glow in the diffuse, romantic light of an English autumn. Among the most imposing of ornamental grasses, these plants can take the place of small trees in the landscape.

LEFT: Many drought-tolerant ornamental grasses are adapted to even the driest climates. Growing alongside native penstemons, this *Muhlenbergia* grass is a wonderful foil for the bold saguaro cacti silhouetted in the background of this Arizona desert garden.

OPPOSITE: Moisture-loving primroses, sedges, and irises make a pleasing foreground mosaic as variegated manna grass, *Glyceria maxima* 'Variegata', ventures out into the water, providing a light contrast with the magenta azalea.

Chapter Four

GRASSES IN NATIVE LANDSCAPES

rasses are an integral part of the drama of contrasting textures, forms, colors, and illumination that is common to many native landscapes. Whether your design preference is formal or informal, an awareness of natural patterns will provide inspiration for integrating grasses into your own landscape.

TOP LEFT: Reminiscent of the once vast midwestern prairies, this autumnal blanket woven from broomsedge, *Andropogon virginicus*, and little bluestem, *Schizachyrium scoparium*, grows naturally in this field on the east coast of the United States.

BOTTOM LEFT: Infused with a golden glow in a sunny autumn meadow, this switch grass, *Panicum virgatum*, is highlighted against the muted forest beyond.

OPPOSITE: These grand sweeps of switch grass, *Panicum virgatum*, followed by the taller common reed, *Phragmites australis*, are the natural result of varying moisture on this sloping ground in New York State. In wild landscapes, grasses frequently occur in masses, and these natural formations are effective models for larger garden designs. The silvery monochrome of the grasses is in sublime balance with the brilliant autumn foliage colors of this East Coast deciduous forest.

ABOVE: Billowy clouds of crinkled hair grass, *Deschampsia flexuosa*, tumble over massive black granite boulders high in the Blue Ridge Mountains. This dynamic combination eloquently suggests similar juxtapositions in the gardened landscape.

LEFT: Even in cold climates, the beauty of wild grasses transcends the dimming effect of winter. Both lithe and resilient, little bluestem, *Schizachyrium scoparium*, recovers here from midwinter snows to paint a hillside with its fawns and russets.

ABOVE: Native to the coastal mountains of southern California, deergrass, *Muhlenbergia rigens*, beautiful-ly adorns distinctive boulders dramatically arrayed among live oaks. The low angle of the late-winter sun impressively sidelights both grass and stone.

ABOVE: Here, huge burnished tufts of *Chionochloa rubra* are splayed by powerful winds sweeping the interior mountains of New Zealand's south island.

Chapter Five

CONTRASTING ELEMENTS

F̵ew gardens consist solely of plants; the most satisfying compositions make imaginative decorative use of other elements. These may be natural or man-made, luxuries or necessities, fixed features or movable objects. Ornamental grasses work well when combined with other elements in the garden, however their airy, fine-textured qualities are especially effective when associated with features of greater density and weight.

STAIRS, STEPS, AND WALKWAYS

RIGHT: This west-facing stone walk leads directly into the setting autumn sun, which splendidly backlights the foliage and flowers of wild oat, *Chasmanthium latifolium.*

OPPOSITE: Whenever possible, build garden walkways wide enough to allow grasses and other border plants to spill over them. Laden with raindrops, the rich mix of grasses and perennials in this intimate English garden have discreetly pushed their way over the cut stone walk.

ABOVE: Soft to the touch as well as to the eye, the arching flowers of these mellic grasses, *Melica ciliata,* complement the curves of this weathered fieldstone walkway.

LEFT: Beginning in the foreground, fountain grass, *Pennisetum alopecuroides, Spodiopogon sibiricus,* and tall moor grass, *Molinia* 'Transparent', alternate with bolder sedums and coneflowers to create a handsomely varied framework for this simple bluestone walk.

ABOVE: This concrete stairway might seem too heavy for this garden if not for the softening effect of the ornamental grasses. Beginning along the pathway, a plumed procession of fountain grass, *Pennisetum orientale;* Korean feather-reed grass, *Calamagrostis arundinacea* var. *brachytricha;* and *Miscanthus* 'Purpurascens' gracefully ascends the stairs. Small containers of scarlet geraniums provide pointed accents of color.

ABOVE RIGHT: The loosely pendulous, illuminated spikelets of wild oat, *Chasmanthium latifolium,* are the perfect complement to the precise stone steps leading over the water in this intimate pool garden.

FENCES, GATES, AND WALLS

ABOVE: Here, the elegant flower stalks of tall moor grass, *Molinia* 'Windspiel', admirably ease the transition from a sturdy white-painted fence to a rustic bridge crossing a small stream just beyond.

LEFT: This doorway dramatically frames a specimen *Miscanthus* 'Purpurascens'. The luminous grass beckons visitors to pass through the portal into the sun-drenched landscape beyond.

ABOVE: A simple split-rail fence takes on a sculptural quality when backed by a solid chestnut-colored sweep of native grasses. The fence might be functional, marking a property line between neighbor's fields, or it might be an artful contrivance used to signal the division between a formal mowed section of garden and a less manicured area deliberately sown with native grasses. In either case, the fallen rail adds a charming bit of disorder.

LEFT: When planted en masse, fountain grasses, *Pennisetum alopecuroides*, and orange coneflowers superbly balance the weight of this solid stone wall.

OPPOSITE: A tidy and neatly contained row of ribbon grass, *Phalaris arundinacea* 'Picta', brightens the base of this dry-laid field-stone wall. The white variegation in the foliage of the grass echoes the white flower puffs of *Fothergilla*.

GARDEN FURNITURE, SCULPTURE, AND ARCHITECTURE

ABOVE: Mature specimens of various *Miscanthus* grasses provide privacy on this otherwise open, sunny stone patio. With the sun's rays lapping at these chaise longues, this secluded hideaway will be cherished as summer breezes whisper through the grasses.

RIGHT: Man-made objects with strong forms, such as this antique iron wheel, create a wonderful dynamic with grasses. Placed here with Indian grass, *Sorghastrum nutans*, and goldenrods in a naturalistic meadow garden, the rusty wheel creates a setting evocative of a pastoral landscape that is all-too-quickly vanishing.

ABOVE: A large *Miscanthus* 'Gracillimus' in full bloom gracefully connects this deck to the ground and water below. The cascading grass acts to accentuate the strong horizontal lines of the porch.

ABOVE: The explosive form of this Korean feather-reed grass, *Calamagrostis arundinacea* var. *brachytricha*, stands in bold contrast with the refined, rounded form of a small gazebo.

ABOVE: This poolside setting showcases feather-reed grass, *Calamagrostis* 'Karl Foerster'. The height of the grass is accentuated by the broad surface of the water and lower-growing coneflowers and fountain grasses, while the masses of crimson barberry and a purple beech behind provide dark contrast with the tawny flowers of the grass.

ABOVE: An allee of pleached linden trees introduces an intriguing horizontal line to this landscape, contrasting with both the steeply pitched roof of the building and the relaxed flowing form of the Korean feather-reed grass, *Calamagrostis arundinacea* var. *brachytricha*. This garden ingeniously intermingles vegetables and traditional ornamental plants: red-stemmed Swiss chard is visible through the feathery plumes of the grass.

STONES

ABOVE: Fountains of blue oat grass, *Helictotrichon sempervirens*, flow freely from stone crevices in this New York State rock garden. Although the scene is entirely contrived, it borrows directly from innumerable natural models where delicate grasses are intermingled with coarse boulders.

DECORATIVE CONTAINERS

ABOVE: The enduring foliage color of ornamental grasses ideally suits them for use in decorative containers. This coal-black urn showcases a brightly variegated *Miscanthus*, providing an imposing focal point at the end of a rich tapestry of flowering herbaceous plants and colorful shrubs.

LEFT: Set against a backdrop of Japanese red maple, this container combination of blue oat grass, *Helictotrichon sempervirens*, and purple setcreasea is satisfying all summer long.

ABOVE: Almost any grass can be displayed in a container if given sufficient space for root development. Here, mature specimens of *Miscanthus* 'Purpurascens' are edged with small blue fescues in these large wooden containers and are still quite beautiful even in late autumn.

LEFT: The wine-red color of this purple fountain grass, *Pennisetum setaceum* 'Rubrum', would be welcome in many areas of the garden and can be easily relocated due to the versatility of this modest-size container.

BOLD-TEXTURED COMPANION PLANTS

ABOVE: This elegant and dramatic combination balances the relatively fine-textured foliage of *Miscanthus* with the gargantuan leaves of *Petasites*.

ABOVE: The most compelling gardens are often created by the apparent collision of disparate styles. Here, immaculately clipped conical yews, the quintessence of formal horticulture, are unusually arresting awash in the informality of *Miscanthus*.

RIGHT: The bold, dried flowers of this ornamental thistle make a stirring combination with the tightly tufted foliage of blue fescue.

ABOVE: In an appealing combination, the delicate autumn plumes of Korean feather-reed grass, *Calamagrostis arundinacea* var. *brachytricha*, lean affectionately on the strong shoulders of a burgundy-colored sedum.

OPPOSITE: Fountains of fine *Pennisetum* foliage are striking when placed opposite the dinner plate–size flower heads and rugged leaves of a cow-parsnip.

67

ABOVE: This needle grass, *Stipa pulchra*, is too subtle to be effective by itself, but in combination with these bright orange California poppies, the grass makes a bold statement in this simple but eye-catching scene.

OPPOSITE: Here, a giant plume poppy towers over a tropically luxuriant specimen of porcupine grass, *Miscanthus* 'Strictus'. The orange coneflowers add a touch of bright color.

ABOVE: Colorful foliage of variegated Hakone grass, *Hakonechloa macra* 'Aureola', blends harmoniously with the bright daisylike flowers of a *Senecio*, while various foliage textures are richly contrasted in this artfully composed border.

OPPOSITE: Experiment with all manners of bold-textured plants when choosing companions for your grasses. These prickly pear cacti are surprisingly successful mates to this variegated *Miscanthus*.

INDEX

Arundo donax, 10, 11, 14, 24, 25
Autumn, grasses in, 16, 17, 32, 42, 43

Barberry, 23, 24, 59
Bluestem (*Schizachyrium scoparium*), 43, 44, 45
Broomsedge (*Andropogan virginicus*), 43
Bulbs, 22

Cacti, 70
Calamagrostis. See Feather-reed grass.
Chasmanthium latifolium, 17, 49, 52
Chionochloa rubra, 47
Clematis, 28, 29
Coneflowers, 31, 32, 37, 50, 55, 69
Containers, 61–62
Cortaderia. See Pampas grass.
Courtyard, 20, 25
Cow-parsnip, 66, 67

Daylilies, 35
Deergrass (*Muhlenbergia*), 40, 46
Deschampsia. See Hair grass.
Desert garden, 40

Feather grass, 38, 39
Feather-reed grass (*Calamagrostis*)
Karl Foerster, 9, 34, 36, 37, 59, 67
Korean, 52, 58, 59
Fences, 53, 55
Fescue
blue, 27, 28, 62, 64, 65
Meerblau, 13

Fountain grass (*Pennisetum*), 22, 23, 24, 28, 29, 50, 51, 52, 55, 66, 67
Rubrum, 62
Foxtail (*Alopecurus pratensis*), 13

Garden design
fences/gates/walls, 52–55
formal, 21–29
furniture/sculpture/architecture, 56–59
informal, 30–41
native plants, 42–47
rock garden, 60
stairways, 52–53
walkways, 24, 29, 35, 48–51
Goldenrod, 56, 57

Hair grass (*Deschampsia*)
crinkled, 45
tufted, 24
Hakone grass, 71
Heather, 13

Indian grass (*Sorghastrum nutans*), 56, 57

Japanese bloodgrass (*Imperata* Red Baron), 13

Koeleria, 20

Lyme grass (*Elymus arenarius*), 35

Manna grass (*Glyceria maxima*), 40, 41
Mellic grass (*M. ciliata*), 8, 9, 35, 51
Miscanthus, 19, 28, 36, 56, 61, 63, 64, 70
Gracillimus, 58
Graziella, 6

Morning Light, 11, 21
Purpurascens, 32, 52, 53, 62
Silberfeder, 38, 39
Strictus, 11, 32, 33, 68, 69
Molinia, 20
Karl Foerster, 12
Transparent, 50, 51
Windspiel, 53
Moor grass. *See Molinia.*
Muhlenbergia. See Deergrass.
Mulleins, 26, 27

Native landscape, 42–47
Needle grass (*Stipa pulchra*), 68
New Zealand grasses, 14, 15, 47

Oat grass
blue, 23, 27, 60, 61
wild, 17, 49, 52
Ornamental grasses. *See also* Garden design.
attributes of, 7, 9
in autumn, 16, 17, 32, 42, 43
companion plants, 11, 12, 13, 23, 31, 36, 63–69
in containers, 61–62
drought-tolerant, 40
in perennial border, 26, 27, 29, 35, 39
variegated, 14
in winter, 18, 19, 44, 45

Pampas grass (*Cortaderia*), 16, 17, 40
Gold Band, 26, 27
Pennisetum. See Fountain grass.
Petasites, 63
Poppies, 68, 69
Porcupine grass, 11, 32, 33, 68, 69

Ravenna grass (*Erianthus r.*), 7
Reed
common (*Phragmites australis*), 42, 43
giant (*Arundo donax*), 10, 11, 14, 24, 25
Ribbon grass (*Phalaris arundinacea*), 39, 54, 55
Rock garden, 60

Sedum, 31, 32, 67
Seed-heads, 17, 19
Senecio, 71
Sesleria, 20
Setcreasea, 61
Spodiopogon sibiricus, 50, 51
Stairways, 52, 53
Switch grass (*Panicum virgatum*), 31, 32, 43

Thistles, 5, 18, 64, 65

Walkways, 24, 29, 35, 48–51
Walls, 20, 54, 55
Water garden, 21, 24, 30, 31, 59
Winter, grasses in, 18, 19, 44, 45

Yew, 64
Yucca, 22, 23, 36

PHOTO CREDITS

All photographs © Rick Darke, with the following exceptions: © John Glover: 16, 18 (both), 39, 40 (top), 41, 71; © Bruce Jenkins/FullFrame: 15; © Charles Mann: 26, 40 (bottom); © Derek Fell: 38, 56, 62; © Cynthia Woodyard: 55 (top).